This book demonstrates the Empathy words:
IMAGINATION, RESPECT, THANKFULNESS, NURTURING, COMPASSION, GRATITUDE, HAPPINESS, KINDNESS & JOYFULNESS.

They have been bolded in the story or included as footnotes to encourage a family dialogue.

Where Is Snoozy? is published and distributed by WRDPLAY Publishing.

Where Is Snoozy? © Copyright 2023 WRDPLAY Publishing

No part of this book may be reproduced in any form or by any means, electronic or mechanical, including photocopying, recording, or by any information storage or retrieval system, without permission in writing from the publisher, except in the case of reprints in the context of reviews. All persons and events in this publication are fictitious. Any similarity to actual persons or events is unintentional. For information please contact WRDPLAY Publishing at 58 Armstrong Street, Ottawa, Ontario Canada K1Y 2B7

ISBN 978-1-998025-00-8

Where is Snoozy?
A Life-Stories Adventure with Noah

"WHERE IS SNOOZY?" sobbed Noah, "He was with me when I went to bed last night!"

"Let's go in your room and look. He has to be close by," said Noah's mom. She knew the much loved brown sloth stuffie could not be far.

They looked in a drawer, on the floor, in the bed and under the bed...BUT NO SNOOZY!

"SEE, I TOLD YOU SNOOZY IS GONE!" cried Noah.

"He is here...somewhere. But this house is a mess. If things are put back where they belong, it would be much easier to find them," his mom calmly replied.

"Psst, I hear you are looking for a missing sloth," inquired Detective Mom. "I believe I can help. What were you doing last night before bed?"

Noah detailed the events of the previous evening: he had played with the police car, got pajamas on, and read a bedtime story.

*Empathy example: Noah's Mom uses her **IMAGINATION** to help him calm down and work towards solving a problem.*

"Hmmm, if we look under those clothes do you think Snoozy could be there?" asked Detective Mom.

So Noah hung up the clothes, closed the drawers, and put a few things away...BUT NO SNOOZY!

Then Noah remembered that the family had been in the living room having a dance party. He put on all the rockstar accessories that were left on the floor, played the piano, tapped the drum, and looked under the couch cushions.
BUT NO SNOOZY!

"The search must have made you hungry. How about a sandwich?" asked Mom, "Can you get the peanut butter for me?"

Noah put the chef's hat on and started looking for the peanut butter. There were lots of things to be found in the kitchen...warm cookies, a kitten, and peanut butter...BUT NO SNOOZY!

After lunch, Noah THANKED his mom for the food and put the dirty dishes in the sink. OOPS! A glass of milk spilled all over his pants.

Additional empathy example: Noah shows RESPECT by thanking his mother for lunch and picking up after himself (the dishes).

Maybe Snoozy is in here, thought Noah. He looked under the dirty clothes and in the cupboards...BUT NO SNOOZY!

It was a beautiful day, so Noah's mom suggested he look outside. Maybe Murphy had taken the sloth into the backyard.

"Oh no, Murphy is terrible with toys!" exclaimed Noah while running into the backyard.

"Did you hide Snoozy?" he quizzed the dog who whined because all he wanted was someone to throw the ball.

Noah did, and the dog was HAPPY.

Additional empathy examples:
Noah shows **KINDNESS** to Murphy by listening to the signs (crying) the dog gives him and reacts **COMPASSIONATELY**.

Spotting the pail and shovel, Noah thought it might be a good idea to put them in the sandbox in case Murphy decided to chew them.

So, he went to the basement, put on a magician's cape, top hat, and grabbed the all important wand.

Empathy example: When Noah uses 'magic' to find Snoozy, it demonstrates **IMAGINATION** as he is hoping for a positive outcome to his problem.

"Abracadabra! 1, 2, 3...
Make my toy appear...so everyone can cheer!"
chanted Noah, and with that he whipped the cloth off the box.

"MOM! Snoozy is back!" declared Noah JOYFULLY. "I retraced my steps, put away my toys, and found him in the playroom. I must have left him there yesterday while we were practicing magic tricks."

Mom was thrilled that Noah had cleaned up and done KIND things for the family's pets. It was definitely time for a reward: a delicious chocolate chip cookie.

After a long and busy day, Noah and Snoozy were together again.

DID YOU SEE...

While looking for Snoozy did you also happen to spot all of Squishy's kittens? There is one to be found on each spread.

Looking for where to buy your very own Snoozy Sloth Stuffie?
Visit https://brighttimetoys.com/

www.ingramcontent.com/pod-product-compliance
Lightning Source LLC
Chambersburg PA
CBHW082021050526
44107CB00100B/600